5/11

ON PARADE

ON PARADE

THE HIDDEN WORLD OF ANIMALS IN ENTERTAINMENT

ONE VOICE

ROB LAIDLAW

Fitzhenry & Whiteside

Published in Canada by
Fitzhenry & Whiteside,
195 Allstate Parkway,
Markham, Ontario L3R 4T8

Published in the United States by
Fitzhenry & Whiteside,
311 Washington Street,
Brighton, Massachusetts 02135

www.fitzhenry.ca   godwit@fitzhenry.ca

Library and Archives Canada Cataloguing in Publication
Laidlaw, Rob
    On parade : the hidden world of animals in entertainment / Rob Laidlaw.
Includes bibliographical references.
ISBN 978-1-55455-143-9
    1. Animal welfare—Juvenile literature. 2. Captive wild animals—Juvenile
literature. 3. Circus animals—Juvenile literature. I. Title.
QL77.5.L328 2010   j636.088'9   C2010-900230-X

U.S. Publisher Cataloging-in-Publication Data (Library of Congress Standards)
Laidlaw, Rob.
On parade : the hidden world of animals in entertainment / Rob Laidlaw.
[48] p. : col. ill., col. photos. ; cm.
Summary: Rob Laidlaw exposes the hidden lives and often inhumane treatment of animals around the world that are trained and kept for the purpose of entertainment.
ISBN: 978-1-55455-143-9
1. Animal welfare – Juvenile literature. 2. Circus animals – Juvenile literature. 2. Captive wild animals—Juvenile literature. I. Title.
636.088/9 dc22   QL77.5.L353 2010

Fitzhenry & Whiteside acknowledges with thanks the Canada Council for the Arts, and the Ontario Arts Council for their support of our publishing program. We acknowledge the financial support of the Government of Canada through the Book Publishing Industry Development Program (BPIDP) for our publishing activities.

Design by Fortunato Design Inc.

Cover photo credits: Zoocheck/www.zoocheck.com

Printed in Hong Kong, China

10 9 8 7 6 5 4 3 2 1

CONTENTS

INTRODUCTION

I'll never forget my first up-close encounter with circus animals. It was back in the early 1990s, when I was a humane society inspector. When I entered the tent where the world-famous Moscow Circus bears were housed, I was shocked. Lined up in front of me were nearly a dozen bears in tiny wooden crates not much larger than the bears themselves. They were all rapidly swinging their heads from side to side. They stared straight ahead, seemingly oblivious to my presence. The circus staff said they stayed in those boxes all the time, except when performing.

More recently in 2009 at a circus in my hometown, I saw three elephants chained to the ground, swaying back and forth. Each elephant was confined to an area about the size of a single-car parking space.

During the past 30 years, I've observed how animals in entertainment are treated around the world. I've seen animals in circuses and traveling shows, television and film productions, aquatic shows and magic acts. I've encountered alligator wrestling, begging street elephants, temple elephants, snakes in baskets, animals used in races and fights, and even some given away as prizes.

Born Free Foundation

The world of animals in entertainment is complex and involves a lot of animals. It's easy to feel overwhelmed by the problems, but don't, because there's good news coming from all over the world.

While I was writing this book, Bolivia banned all animals in circuses. A number of advertising agencies in the United States said they wouldn't use chimpanzees and orangutans in their publicity campaigns any more. I also received an email with news that two greyhound tracks in the US hosted their last races in December 2009.

There are now hundreds of organizations and thousands of private individuals, many of them kids, speaking out on behalf of animals in entertainment. As a director of the wildlife protection organization Zoocheck Canada, part of my job involves working to alleviate animal suffering and trying to stop the exploitation of animals in entertainment.

I believe all animals should be treated with respect and kindness. I hope this book inspires you to try to make our world a better place for animals. Once you start, you'll find out you really can make a difference.

CHAPTER 1

What All Animals Need

All animals need food, water, and shelter, but other things are essential to good animal welfare, too.

Space

Rachel Plotkin

It's important for all animals to have as much space as possible.

Nearly all animals need room to roam so they can walk, run, climb, fly or swim naturally. Animals in the wild often travel long distances. Coyotes, wolves and bears can travel hundreds of kilometers in a matter of days. Elephants and killer whales may travel thousands of kilometers every year. Even small creatures like insects, reptiles and pocket-sized mammals often need very large living spaces.

Freedom of Choice

Animals make lots of decisions. Their lives are not just guided by instinct. Some decisions they make are minor, such as whether to walk to the right or left of a rock. Others are major decisions, such as where to go to find water during a drought. They think about what they want to do and then they decide to do it. All animals need control over their own lives and an ability to make decisions.

Family

Many animals in the wild live in social groups—in pairs, families, troops, herds and pods. Being part of a group can be a survival advantage because there are more eyes and ears to watch out for danger. A group can also provide protection, such as when several elephant mothers stand over their babies when predators are near.

Groups may also forage for food or hunt cooperatively. Chimpanzees form parties to hunt monkeys. Some dolphins and whales group together to trap schools of fish and then take turns eating them.

Living in a natural group also gives animals comfort and security, as well as opportunities to share resources and knowledge and to learn from each other. It makes life more interesting.

Rob Laidlaw

Things to Do

Most animals are active and spend their days exploring, foraging, hunting, finding mates, solving problems, building nests and dens, protecting their home, communicating, socializing, playing—the list of activities goes on.

Polar bears walk long distances in search of seals. Wild alligators swim, dive, explore, and hunt. Elephants forage and keep active for up to 20 hours a day. They're nothing like their bored counterparts in captivity.

Having things to do increases physical fitness and keeps the minds of animals active. It's now known that animals want to be active and there are scientific studies that prove it.

The Lion's Pace and Elephant's Sway

When animals can't live naturally, boredom, fear, frustration, stress and abnormal behaviors often result. Elephants bob their heads up and down or sway back and forth. Tigers pace the same pattern in their cages. Bears weave their heads from side to side. Giraffes endlessly lick whatever they can reach. These odd behaviors show that animals aren't coping very well. Sitting still, lying down, or sleeping all the time are also signs that something is wrong.

Animal Defenders International

CHAPTER 2

Circus Performers

The World's Greatest Elephant

This large grey statue weighing 38 tons is perched above the highway as you enter the City of St. Thomas, Ontario, Canada. Erected in 1985, it commemorates the life and death of Jumbo the elephant.

Rob Laidlaw

Jumbo was born in 1861 in a remote desert region of Africa. He never strayed far from his mother or family. His pillar-like legs and cushioned feet were made for long-distance, energy-efficient walking, and his home range was hundreds of square kilometers in size.

In the wild, Jumbo would have known dozens, maybe even hundreds, of other elephants during his lifetime. He'd communicate with them through body movements, chemical signals, vibrations in the ground, and sounds, including low frequency rumbles that only other elephants can hear, even many kilometers away. But when he was just a year old, a band of elephant hunters, hired to collect animals for exhibitions and zoos in Europe, targeted his family.

The hunters were being paid to collect two elephant calves and there was only one way to do it. They charged the herd. Little Jumbo couldn't run very fast and was soon separated from the others. His mother tried to chase the hunters away, but they quickly killed her with their swords. Jumbo stood perfectly still, afraid to move.

The hunters forced Jumbo to make a long walk across the desert. Lacking his mother's milk, Jumbo was soon thin and sickly. He survived, but another baby elephant making the journey died on the way.

Jumbo was then transported by train to Alexandria and by ship to Germany to be part of a traveling show called the Grand Menagerie. Later he was sold to the zoo in Paris where he lived in a cramped, concrete pen. In 1865, he was sold to the London Zoo.

Soon Jumbo was the largest elephant in captivity. He gave rides to children. But as he got older, he became aggressive, so the London Zoo sold him to P.T. Barnum, owner of the Barnum and Bailey Circus in the United States. He arrived in New York in April 1882. His job involved little more than walking in front of circus spectators, but his fame grew with every show.

On September 15, 1885, after a circus performance in St. Thomas, Ontario, Canada, Jumbo was being walked back to his holding area, in the dark of night, along a railway track. An unscheduled freight train barrelled toward him. Unwilling to walk down a steep embankment, Jumbo just stood there refusing to move. The train hit his rear legs, knocked him on his side, and pushed him down the tracks. He died a short while later.

P.T. Barnum called Jumbo a hero. He said he died trying to save Tom Thumb, another smaller elephant that was nearby when Jumbo was hit. The story wasn't true, but it helped Barnum inflate the Jumbo legend even more.

Barnum had Jumbo's skin stuffed and mounted and his skeleton reconstructed. They were then pulled on trailers around the circus ring to a background of funeral music. The other elephants marched behind, veiled in black. Even in death, Jumbo was exploited to generate a profit.

Life on the Road

© Animal Defenders International

Cramped transport and living conditions don't provide the physical and mental stimulation all elephants need.

A growing number of towns and cities around the world have prohibited performing wild animals within their boundaries.

PETA

In August 1997, police officers in New Mexico noticed a King Royal Circus trailer parked on the highway rocking back and forth. Inside the sweltering, filthy truck was Heather, a young African elephant, dead on the floor. Two other elephants and eight llamas were also crammed into the poorly ventilated space. The temperature inside was estimated to be about 49° C (120° F).

It's common for animals being moved around by truck or rail car to be confined in spaces not much larger than they are. They're small because you don't want animals shifting around in moving vehicles. Unfortunately many animals spend a great deal of their lives in travel cages.

In 2000, a humane society in eastern Canada encountered three elephants crammed into a trailer, along with a number of ponies. Two of the elephants' heads were pressed against the wire barrier separating them from the ponies. The elephant facing forward had her head pushed up against the front wall of the trailer. Nearly 12 hours later, the animals hadn't moved.

Three brown bears touring with a circus in Ontario had it even worse. They had become difficult to handle, so for nearly ten months they lived in the back of a truck and never got out.

Documents filed by animal welfare groups in a legal action against Ringling Bros. Circus say elephants were chained in rail cars for an average of 20 hours when traveling from one venue to another, and were often kept in box cars for 60 to 70 hours and sometimes as much as 90 to 100 hours. Imagine being chained in one spot from Thursday night to Monday night.

Chains

Chaining elephants in circuses and traveling shows is common. They're usually chained by one front leg and one rear leg in an area about the size of one or two parking lot spaces. In a 2009 paper in the scientific journal *Animal Welfare*, the authors said the elephants in the circuses they reviewed were chained 12–23 hours a day; four circuses kept elephants chained in areas measuring just 7–12 sq. meters (75–129 sq. ft.). That's smaller than a single-car parking space. The elephants could only move 1–2 meters (3.2–6.5 ft.), the length of their chains.

Investigations by the British group Animal Defenders uncovered elephants who spent up to 98% of each day in chains. Another investigation into circuses in India found many elephants chained for more than 20 hours each day.

Some circuses, when space and time permit, construct fenced compounds at performance venues. These are often just small sectioned-off areas of a parking lot, arena floor or, sometimes, an adjacent grassy area. The elephants I've observed in these compounds usually just stand around or shuffle a few steps here and there.

© Animal Defenders International

Wild elephants don't stay in one place; they walk long distances and can be active for up to 20 hours a day.

Vancouver Humane Society

Chained behind a performance venue, this elephant desperately tries to touch the only natural objects within reach. Traveling elephants experience unnatural lives that are boring, frustrating and regimented.

Tethers and Stalls

Hoofed animals may spend most of their time in a small makeshift stall or tied in one spot by a short leash.

Hoofed mammals, called ungulates, are often found in circus collections. The most common is the horse, but there may also be camels, zebras, giraffes and rhinos.

The hoofed animals I've seen were usually confined in tiny hard-floored stalls hardly longer than they were. I've also seen them tied by a short leash, sometimes as short as one meter, to a fence, trailer, or piece of equipment.

At the Great British Circus in 2006, Animal Defenders found that over a three day observation period two horses, two ponies, four reindeer, four llamas and five camels were not walked or exercised beyond their brief appearances in the ring.

With their natural movements and behaviors severely restricted or eliminated, ungulates become bored, frustrated, or stressed. Many develop abnormal behaviors, such as excessive licking, barrier biting, or tongue playing.

Beast Wagons

A big cat or bear living in a beast wagon is like a human living in a closet. Even dangerous criminals are treated better and many of them eventually get out.

Big cats, bears, apes and other animals are often kept in small, wheeled cages called beast wagons. They sometimes measure just 1.2-1.5m (4-5 ft) wide by 2.4-3.04m (8-10 ft) long. The animals have to eat, sleep, defecate and urinate in that small space.

In British circuses, it's common to find long, thin steel cages permanently fixed onto the backs of trucks. Animal Defenders found big cats living in such cages 75-99% of the time.

After my visit to the Moscow Circus, they constructed a larger exercise cage measuring about 3.05m (10 ft) by 3.05m (10 ft). Each bear spent a few hours a week in the cage, but there was nothing to do, so they just sat there. It didn't really make a difference.

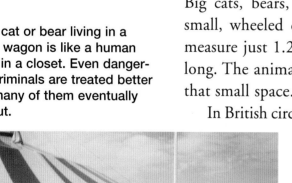

Rest and Relaxation?

What happens to performing animals when they're not traveling? Show operators often talk about spacious, natural enclosures at their home bases or winter quarters where the animals can rest and relax, but the reality is usually quite different.

A 1996 investigation of the UK Chipperfield Circus winter quarters found animals living in filthy conditions. Veterinarian Samantha Scott said the accommodation for the elephant and giraffes showed a serious lack of knowledge, care, or both.

The Hawthorn Corporation, a company that supplied elephants to circuses, was charged by the United States Department of Agriculture for violations of the Animal Welfare Act. The company paid a fine of $200,000 for keeping animals in poor conditions at their home base and agreed to give up all sixteen of their elephants.

Animals in some independently-owned acts or shows that are in high demand may get no rest and relaxation. Once they're done with one show or tour, they just move on to another.

Animal accommodation may be very small, even when the animals are not on the road.

15

Breeding and Babies

Some people claim that breeding captive elephants in the circus is good for elephant conservation. It seems to me that breeding elephants may be good for circuses but not too helpful to conservation because it's unlikely any of these elephants will ever be returned to the wild. Besides, elephants have no problem breeding and producing calves in the wild. They just need to be kept safe from poachers and to have their remaining habitat protected.

Learning Isn't Always Fun

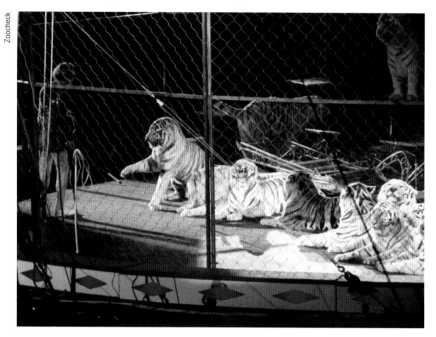

There are many different kinds of training, but they all take place in private before an animal is put in front of an audience.

"When you hear that screaming, you know you got their attention." These words were caught on an undercover videotape of an elephant-training session at the Carson & Barnes Circus in 1999. The videotape shows the circus's animal care director beating elephants with a bullhook and an electric prod. The director cautions his trainees that elephants must not be punished in front of the public. I think most people would agree

The Ankus (Bullhook)

The ankus is a wooden, metal or fiberglass stick with a metal hook and point on one end. It's a standard tool carried by elephant trainers. The hook or point of the ankus is applied to a sensitive part of the elephant's body, such as behind the ears, on the face or behind the legs. The elephant doesn't like it, so they move away in the direction the trainer intends. It's supposed to be used gently and only as a guide. Unfortunately, many trainers have been observed using it as a weapon, poking and stabbing elephants with the ankus, puncturing or tearing their skin in the process, and hitting them on the head and behind the legs. Many parts of an elephant's skin are thin and sensitive, so it's easy to cause pain.

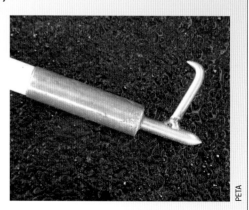

Sarah Baeckler Undercover

In 2002 Sarah Baeckler volunteered for a program offered by one of Hollywood's biggest animal suppliers. She wanted to investigate how ape actors were treated and thought a program that taught her how to be an animal trainer would be a great place to start. She spent more than a year at the facility for one to three days each week.

Sarah said she saw "sickening acts of emotional, psychological and physical abuse every single day on the job." She encountered trainers punching and kicking chimps, hitting them with sticks, and throwing rocks and other hard objects at them, even at the babies.

Her investigation led to a lawsuit that resulted in the chimps being turned over to a sanctuary.

that this type of animal treatment is wrong, so it is not surprising that trainers wouldn't want everyone to see what they are doing.

Similarly, on the People for the Ethical Treatment of Animals (PETA) website, a 2009 undercover investigation video shows handlers at the Ringling circus repeatedly hitting elephants with bullhooks on the head, face, and body, and striking tigers with whips. In July 2009, the group filed a criminal cruelty-to-animals complaint with the City of Philadelphia District Attorney against the circus.

Pat Derby, former Hollywood animal trainer and co-founder of the Performing Animal Welfare Society (PAWS), said that during her career she saw elephants being beaten and electro-shocked, bears' noses being broken and their feet burned, and big cats being struck with wooden bats. Some of those abuses still go on today.

But why would trainers treat their animals so badly? In the world of entertainment, the animals' ability to perform the right action at the right time is what makes those animals valuable to their trainers. If they don't perform on cue, they won't get hired. That's a strong reason for trainers or handlers to "make" their animals perform. Their livelihood may depend on it. As well, some people still believe it's appropriate and necessary to hit animals, such as elephants, for control purposes. I think if you have to hit animals to keep control, then maybe you shouldn't be keeping those animals.

Most animal trainers claim that things are different now and that mistreatment is rare. Maybe it's sometimes possible to train animals humanely, and there are probably some trainers who are thoughtful and responsible, but a growing mountain of evidence suggests that these cases are the exception, especially when wild animals are involved.

CHAPTER 3

Movie Stars & Television Celebrities

At least 100 horses were killed during the filming of the 1924 movie *Ben Hur*. During the 1931 filming of the African adventure film *Trader Horn*, lions were starved to make them attack other animals. One early short film screened in theatres even showed an elephant named Topsy being electrocuted. Eventually, the growing number of animals being abused or killed in early film productions prompted people to demand laws that would protect animal actors.

When television became popular in the 1940s and 1950s, the numbers of animals used in entertainment increased even more. Some animal actors became famous, including Cheetah the chimpanzee in the 1960s *Tarzan* television series, Flipper the dolphin, the dogs Rin Tin Tin, Lassie and Benji, Elsa the lion, Babe the pig, Flicka the horse, Sammy the orangutan from *Dunstan Checks In* and the chimps from the *Most Valuable Primate* movies. There are also hundreds of other not-so-famous animals.

Renting out animals for film productions and television commercials can be very profitable. Animal suppliers and zoos sometimes charge hundreds or even thousands of dollars to rent an animal for just one day.

Unfortunately, many animal actors are kept in small cages and enclosures when they're not on the set being filmed. I've observed animals kept in undersized, bland, boring cages in several film supply facilities.

Hazina the baby hippo starred in a Christmas advertising campaign for a Canadian telecommunications company. She was extremely cute, so the ads became very popular. In 2006, the British Columbia

Performing Animal Welfare Society

18

SPCA recommended to government lawyers that they file a charge of cruelty to animals against the zoo that supplied Hazina for the commercials. They said she had been kept alone for 19 months in an inadequate enclosure with little access to sunlight and a pool so shallow she couldn't float, causing strain to her legs and joints. The SPCA also said the zoo had repeatedly promised to improve her conditions, but they made little effort to actually do so.

In 2007, the government lawyer who controlled the case dropped the charges against the zoo because the zoo had finally built a new enclosure. The SPCA wanted to proceed with the prosecution, but there was nothing the organization could do. It was out of their hands.

Some high profile advertising agencies have pledged not to use live animals, such as great apes. Other companies have stopped using live animals altogether. So progress is being made. An exciting development is the use of computer-generated animals for commercials. Frank and Gordon, two computer-generated beavers, have helped to promote cell phones for Bell Canada. Animated polar bears are helping to sell Coke.

Today, the technology exists that will allow the entertainment industry to remove live animals from film and television productions completely. As this technology continues to improve and become more accessible, I hope we see a day when the only animals used in films, television, and commercials are computer-generated.

In April 2009, an English falconer whose owls appeared in the Harry Potter movies pled guilty to 17 charges of cruelty.
A veterinarian who examined the falconer's home base described the birds' living conditions as "filthy" and "squalid."

No Animals Were Harmed!

At the end of movies where animals have been used, you'll often see the statement "no animals were harmed in the making of this film." It means the film has satisfied the American Humane Association's *Guidelines for the Safe Use of Animals in Filmed Media*. Look for it the next time you go to the movies or watch a video at home.

AHA officials are on the set during filming to check that the guidelines are being followed and that no animals are being harmed. While the guidelines have certainly minimized animal abuse, some animal welfare groups point out that the guidelines only deal with animals when they are actually on the set. They do not oversee the pre-production training when most of the abuse happens. Furthermore, these groups argue that the AHA doesn't have the proper authority to enforce the guidelines and deal with problems.

The Wild World of Nature Shows

Lemmings are solitary rodents by nature. They thrive in harsh, northern climates.

For more than 100 years, scenes of animals feeding, hunting, and fighting have been featured in all kinds of nature films and shows. Many of these scenes have been staged, so they do not accurately reflect the real lives of animals in the wild. The 1932 film *Bring 'Em Back Alive* contained a scene in which a tiger and python fought each other. In the wild, they would avoid each other, but they had no choice during this fabricated scene. I expect one or both of them suffered injuries. Today, some filmmakers lure animals to film sites and feature unnatural scenes like feeding frenzies. In other instances, the hosts of the shows chase and capture animals to make the show appear more sensational or to add an element of danger.

The 1958 Disney documentary *White Wilderness* contains what is probably the most famous piece of fakery ever. Ironically, though the documentary attempted to "educate" its audience, it ended up reinforcing the commonly held—but mistaken—belief that lemmings commit mass suicide by jumping off cliffs.

The film-makers state that when a lemming population becomes too large, a group will split off and migrate to a new territory. Some will swim out into the ocean, thinking that the large body of water is just a lake, hoping to find a new habitat on the other shore. When they cannot reach the other side, the lemmings drown. But to illustrate the point, the film-makers brought their lemmings, guinea-pig-like Arctic rodents, to a cliff in Alberta, Canada. There, they staged a dramatic re-enactment of the same error they were trying to correct: They filmed the lemmings from various angles to create the impression of a mass migration and forced the herd to tumble over the edge of the cliff. The commentary states that they were going over the cliff, not in an attempt to commit suicide, but to get the ocean below (though in Alberta, with no natural coastline, it would have been a lake). In the end, many lemmings were injured and killed, and the most memorable moment of the film—when the lemmings still jump over a cliff—did nothing to change people's understanding of the lemming and its migration patterns.

I don't know why this sensationalized scene was fabricated; perhaps the film-makers thought it would add excitement. What's really interesting is the fact that, in spite of its inaccuracies, *White Wilderness* won an Academy Award for "Best Documentary Feature."

Faking an occasional scene might not be a big concern when compared to other ways in which animals are exploited. However, we should always be watchful because, as in the case of these lemmings, history has shown that staging animal sequences sometimes involves abuse and may give people distorted information about animals.

Odd, Unusual and Not Always Pretty

Reality TV Animals

Television reality shows are one place where many of the odd, unusual, and not-always-pretty animals (like snakes, rats, bats, cockroaches and crabs) are exploited for entertainment. One of the most controversial shows in recent years was *Fear Factor*. From 2001 until 2006 numerous versions of the show aired around the world.

Contestants on the American show competed against each other for a $50,000 prize. One regular challenge involved creatures and situations that contestants found gross, such as being covered in live crabs, spiders, rats, or snakes, or eating small, living creatures. Can you imagine how horrible it must be for any animal to be eaten alive?

In a foreign version of the show, hundreds of snakes were dumped onto contestants lying in a coffin-like box. One terrified woman grabbed the snakes and tossed them away. They hit the hard edges of the box or landed on the concrete floor. Several contestants repeated this stunt. Snakes bruise easily and have fragile bones. I expect many of them were injured and some were probably crushed when the contestants moved around.

Courtesy of Colin Ybarra/Creative Commons License

Cockroaches have shown the ability to make complex, group-based decisions.

Small, not-so-pretty animals can often suffer just as much as other animals do. Many of them play critical ecological roles in nature. Instead of abusing them for entertainment, we should be teaching people how unique and important they are.

Novelty Animals

Paying a fee to have your photo taken beside a novelty animal, like this bat, supports their exploitation.

A national exhibition with shows, exhibits, rides and games takes place in my hometown of Toronto every summer. One year I learned about a midway game that was giving away live green iguanas as prizes. These lizards are difficult to care for. I'll bet most of them died quickly, innocent victims of a silly game.

In 2006, at the Six Flags Over Georgia amusement park in the USA, visitors who ate a live hissing cockroach could jump to the front of the ride lines. A year later the park added a "Wheel of Fright" where participants ate live worms, cockroaches and crickets. It was meant to be fun and gross, but it was done at the expense of the animals. In a Taiwanese zoo I saw pig races. The human audience seemed to enjoy the show, but I don't know how much the pigs liked it.

The saddest novelty animal I've encountered was a flying fox (a large tropical bat) in a market next to the Tanah Lot Temple in Bali, Indonesia. That poor bat hung upside down on a metal stand while throngs of noisy tourists walked by. He had been disabled, so he couldn't fly away. For a small fee, visitors could feed him a piece of fruit.

Rot Laidlaw

Traveling Reptile Shows

In 2009 I spoke at a college fair. Down the hall, on several tables, reptiles were being displayed in buckets, plastic containers, and bags. None had proper space, shelter, rest areas, light, or heat, and they all showed signs of stress. Turtles sat motionless with their heads, legs, and tails pulled in, or frantically tried to escape from deep, narrow containers. The smallest turtles struggled when they were picked up and turned over, so bystanders could see their hard undersides. Big snakes were paraded around for people to touch. The handlers didn't seem to know that reptiles may perceive handling as a predatory attack or need a rest break after being handled so their metabolism can return to normal. Unfortunately, reptiles don't whimper or cry like other animals do, so their suffering often goes unnoticed.

Reptiles often experience stress and suffering when they're transported and handled, yet traveling reptile shows are still very common.

In most traveling reptile shows, the presenters pass on a few simple facts about the animals and call it "educational." They often allow spectators to touch and handle the "creepy" creatures. But when a reptile is used in a show, spectators often leave with the impression that reptiles make good pets and are easy to care for—especially now that they have seen that many reptiles aren't as scary as they thought. But the truth is that reptiles aren't easy to care for properly. So rather than providing a truly educational experience for the public—one that explains the way that reptiles really live in their native environments, without causing harm to the creatures they are promoting—these popular traveling shows usually just promote the destructive reptile pet trade and make money for the presenters.

23

Rob Laidlaw

Rob Laidlaw

Wings of Entertainment

Parrot shows and raptor demonstrations (involving eagles, hawks and owls) are the most common kinds of bird entertainment. Parrot shows are often presented on a table-top or stage. While a presenter talks, the birds perform tricks. Their wings have often been clipped to prevent flying. In most raptor demonstrations the birds fly around for a few minutes, chase a lure, and then sit on the handler's arm. Many birds are kept in small cages, tied to stands, or staked to the ground when they're not performing.

In Chandler, Arizona, ostrich races feature riders mounted on the birds or being pulled in a chariot. Since birds aren't as solidly built as other kinds of animals, carrying a rider or pulling a heavy load is stressful and may cause injuries to the ostriches, including broken bones, especially if they trip and fall

I've watched wild parrots flying over the rainforest and along riverbanks. They're highly social creatures who sometimes congregate in large flocks. They're also enormously intelligent, able to solve problems, learn from each other, and communicate with other parrots. They're nothing like the birds I've observed in shows, who are always performing simple, silly tricks.

CHAPTER 4

Animals in Entertainment Around the World

Savitha Nagabhushan/ CUPA Bangalore

Savitha Nagabhushan/ CUPA Bangalore

I've traveled all around the world and almost everywhere I go, I encounter animals being used to entertain humans. Some of these situations don't seem too bad for the animals (such as swimming with a dolphin), but if you look closer you'll usually see that the lives of the animals aren't very good at all. I've listed just a few of the other kinds of animal entertainment I've come across over the years. They're ones that you might encounter while on holiday, or maybe even in your hometown. If you do, think about what the lives of animals might be like.

Approximately 190 Indian temples keep elephants to attract tourists or to rent for parades and special events. More than 2,500 other elephants are owned by private individuals who use them to make money on the street. Many are malnourished, injured and in poor shape.

25

Zoo and Wildlife Park Shows

Animals perform in zoo and wildlife park shows around the world. At Sri Racha Tiger Zoo in Thailand, cats jump through flaming hoops and roll over, while elephants perform front leg stands and walk on tightropes. In North America, visitors can ride an elephant or camel, or have their photo taken with a monkey. Some Chinese zoos feature live feeding shows where chickens, pigs, and cows are put in with lions and tigers. Visitors watch the cats try to kill their prey. Zoos claim these shows are educational, but the ones I've seen seem entirely focused on making people laugh or giving them a thrill.

Holly Penfound

CASE STUDY: Lota the Elephant

Lota was born in 1951, captured, separated from her family and shipped to an American zoo when she was four. She was chained for up to 18 hours a day and subjected to force and punishment. Lota challenged the lead position of another elephant named Tamara, so in 1990 she was sold for $1 to the Hawthorn Corporation, a company that supplied elephants to circuses.

When it came time to be moved, Lota was afraid to enter the trailer, so she was beaten and dragged. Her chains broke and she fell backwards, sliding beneath the trailer. The incident was videotaped and generated international outrage.

Lota performed for the next thirteen years. In 1996, she was put into quarantine along with fifteen other Hawthorn elephants, because of fears they had contracted tuberculosis (TB) after two Hawthorn elephants died from the disease while on the road. They spent the next year in the Hawthorn barn.

In June 2001, the United States Department of Agriculture (USDA) found Lota was excessively thin, with sunken eyes and protruding spine and hip bones. Her condition worsened. In October, she was severely ema-

ciated, and a large, painful, fluid-filled sore extended down her thigh. She was infected with TB. The circus that rented her was charged with eighteen violations of the Animal Welfare Act. They pled guilty in 2004.

The USDA filed charges against Hawthorn for violations of the Animal Welfare Act, including causing elephants physical harm and discomfort. Owner John Cuneo gave up all sixteen elephants. Lota and another elephant, Misty, were sent to The Elephant Sanctuary, a 2,700 acre natural habitat refuge in Tennessee.

Rodeo Events

After a Vancouver Humane Society campaign, the City of Vancouver became the first major city to prohibit rodeos.

Rodeos can be found throughout Canada, the United States, Latin America and even Australia. They usually feature a series of timed events, involving horses or other farmed animals that are designed to test the skills of the human participants. These events can include calf roping, barrel racing, bull and bareback-bronco riding and steer wrestling to name a few. While rodeo associations claim their activities are not cruel, many animal welfare groups point to the fact that some of the animals are jumped on, pulled around and thrown to the ground. One of the most controversial rodeo events are chuckwagon races in which a team of horses pull a wagon around a track. A number of horses have been killed during chuckwagon races.

Photo Sessions

At tourist destinations around the world people pay to have their photos taken with a monkey, baby big cat, or other animals. In shopping malls, fairs and special events in Canada and the US, dangerous adult big cats are used for photos. In some Asian zoos, visitors can even have their photo taken while they sit on the back of a chained tiger or lion, a practice that is both abusive and dangerous.

Snakes, Alligators & Traveling Shows

Hundreds of thousands of snake charmers practice their trade on the streets of India. The venomous snakes may have had their fangs removed or have been mutilated in other ways to render them harmless. Alligator wrestling shows are popular in parts of the United States and several other countries. Traveling animal shows featuring all kinds of creatures are common in North American schools, at special events and at fairs.

Magic Shows

Magic acts are popular around the world, especially in major tourist destinations like Las Vegas, USA. Some shows feature dangerous animals, such as tigers, who perform without proper safety barriers, just a few feet from audience members. Other animals, like parrots, are often used as props in magic shows, usually for just a few minutes at a time, and then kept in small cages or on stands.

Snake charming has been outlawed in India for decades, but the practice persists.

CASE STUDY: The Suarez Seven

In 1997, a biologist wrote to me describing the conditions of polar bears in the Suarez Bros. Circus. "All bears were exposed to direct sunlight and did not have access to water, complete shade or food. At intermittent intervals, a man would spray water on the polar bears…When the water contacted the bears, they would literally convulse…my words cannot begin to describe the horror of this situation."

Later, a Canadian tourist wrote, "…Two of the polar bears were very aggressive and started to fight with each other due to the lack of space…One of the trainers began beating on one of the polar bears with a metal rod which was sharpened to a point at one end…The trainer continued to beat the polar bear's injured paw…The bear was limping with that paw off of the ground…Putting these animals to sleep would be much kinder than enduring this constant pain and abuse."

The circus toured throughout Central America, where animal welfare laws are particularly weak. In June 2001, the circus entered Puerto Rico (part of the US), after receiving an import permit from the US Fish and Wildlife Service (USFWS).

An inspection found the bears living in terrible conditions and one bear named Alaska in horrible shape. The Puerto Rican Department of Natural Resources filed cruelty charges against the circus in August. The judge in the case decided the circus was not guilty.

In March 2002, after learning the circus had provided false Information about Alaska, the USFWS seized her.

Zoocheck/ www.zoocheck.com

The circus moved on to other countries, but none of those countries let the remaining six bears in, so they were left in Puerto Rico. Conditions there got worse.

People for the Ethical Treatment of Animals, the Humane Society of the United States, members of US Congress, and others spoke out for the bears. That led to the USFWS seizing the remaining six animals citing improper permits and violations of the Marine Mammal Protection Act.

One bear died, the result of years of abuse in the circus, but the other bears are now doing better in their new homes.

Rob Laidlaw

Aquariums, Marine Parks and Swim-with-the-Dolphins

Many whales, dolphins, sea lions and seals that perform in aquatic shows have been captured in the wild. When not performing, the animals may be kept in tiny, barren off-exhibit areas. Among the newest, most profitable and abusive marine entertainment fads are dolphin encounters (feeding) and Swim-with-the-Dolphin programs.

Swim-With-The-Dolphin (SWTD) Programs

According to one survey, 80% of people want to swim with dolphins. While swimming with dolphins may seem harmless, even eco-friendly, it supports a cruel industry focused on making money at the animals' expense.

Being captured from the wild and removed from their families is traumatic. Some dolphins die during capture, while others die weeks or months later. The survivors face a life of stress and suffering.

Cathy Kinsman, a specialist who has studied both captive dolphins and wild beluga whales says, "Although it may seem like fun for the people when a dolphin totes a steady line-up of human cargo around her pool day after day, it is an endless job for the dolphin who receives little more than dead fish and a lot of stress."

SWTD programs are growing in number. They're mostly unregulated and unmonitored, so dolphin care varies widely. (So do safety measures for the visitors who participate.) Many SWTD programs keep dolphins in small shallow tanks or sea pens, fenced bays or coves. Their living spaces are incredibly small and boring, compared to the ocean.

Since dolphins can't move their faces, they always look like they're smiling. Maybe that's why people don't see their suffering.

CHAPTER 5

More Animals in Entertainment

To the Finish Line: Racing Animals

Greyhound Athletes

When I was young I visited a dog-racing track in Scotland during a family vacation. I didn't know about the dark underside of this form of animal entertainment. I had no idea that even though greyhounds are made for running, career-ending and even life-threatening injuries can occur, especially if it's too hot or too cold, or if the dogs are pushed too hard. They can suffer heart attacks, sudden collapse before and after racing, spinal cord paralysis and a range of minor injuries. Greyhound protection groups, like Grey2K USA and the Greyhound Protection League, say this happens to thousands of dogs every year; behind the scenes, thousands of greyhounds are kept confined in tiny cages, sometimes barely large enough for them to stand up in.

Dog racing is closely tied to gambling. If dogs aren't profitable because they're too old or injured, they may be killed. Their racing lives may last only a few years. Puppies that show signs of weakness or stunted growth may be destroyed. No one knows how many dogs are killed annually, but it's probably in the thousands.

Greyhound Protection League

Even though greyhounds are made for running, career-ending and even life-threatening injuries can occur if the dogs are pushed too hard.

30

Greyhound Protection League

Dog protection groups say that about 1,000 greyhounds are required to keep a commercial track operating. Large numbers of new racing dogs need to be bred on a regular basis. It's a repeated cycle of breeding, abuse and death to generate a profit.

In the US and other areas, dog racing is declining. Some US states, like Maine, Nevada, Pennsylvania and Massachusetts, have banned the sport. Some members of the dog-racing industry now work with greyhound rescue groups to find homes for retired dogs. That's great news for those dogs, but there are many more that still need help.

Horse Racing

Equestrian (horse) sports such as thorough-bred and standardbred racing, show jumping, dressage, and endurance riding, are popular around the world. Winning horses and their riders often become international celebrities. But equestrian sports have a dark side that includes questionable breeding practices, widespread drug use and the disposal of large numbers of horses to the slaughter industry.

Race horses need to be powerful, but sleek and fast as well, so they are bred for stocky, muscular bodies and spindly legs that can make them vulnerable to breakdowns. They can start racing when they're just two years old, so their skeletons are barely strong enough to endure the pounding they experience on the track.

Information released by the Jockey Club from their new horse injury database showed 2.04 thoroughbred horse deaths per 1,000 starts. That's approximately 780 deaths per year or 15 fatal injuries per week. Another report said more than 1,200 horses died at US tracks in 2008 alone.

Fatal injuries are nothing new in horse-racing. Way back in 1928, famed thoroughbred Black Gold broke down, finished his

Steeplechase is an obstacle course style of horse racing.

During a 2008 trip to the US, I was lucky enough to see small bands of wild mustangs moving across a massive, dry grass plain in northern Nevada. They didn't look or behave like the captive horses I've seen. They looked more natural and alive.

race, and then was euthanized right on the track. Even elite race horses receiving the very best of veterinarian care have broken down during races. In 2008, Eight Belles broke both ankles during the Kentucky Derby.

One increasing problem in equestrian sports, at all levels of competition, is drug use. All kinds of drugs and medications are used in equestrian sports. Many of them are legal, while others, especially performance enhancing substances, are banned. After their horses tested positive for banned substances, several 2004 Olympic medal winners, including a show jumping gold medalist, had to forfeit their awards. The rules for drugs are inconsistent, however, and vary from one jurisdiction to the next. Furthermore, there is a fine line between drugs used as part of veterinary care and drugs used to enhance performance. One group is the steroidal anti-inflammatory drugs. They're usually used in joints to decrease inflammation, something that many horses experience. But what often ends up happening is that injured horses are given steroids to allow them to race, rather than being rested.

One of the biggest problems with horse sports is that thousands of horses are produced each year to fill the vacancies created when the horses before them are no longer useful. With a potential lifespan of 30 years, some race horses have careers that only last 4 or 5 years. After that, they may be shipped to a slaughterhouse or sold to inexperienced owners who can't handle high-strung race horses.

According to the horse protection group Equine Advocates (EA), more than 120,000 horses from the US are supplied to the slaughter industry every year. They are sent to Canada and Mexico because there are currently no horse slaughterhouses in the United States. EA says a substantial number of these horses come from the racing industry.

Some people involved in equestrian sports recognize the problems and have started to take action. They're pushing for humane breeding policies and better rules for drugs. They also know far too many horses are being produced and that they shouldn't be sent to slaughter. Several equine rescue centers for retired horses have been established and there are even adoption programs for retired race horses. These kinds of initiatives are a great step forward for horses, but we still have a lot more to do.

THE BLOODSPORTS

Bloodsports involve forcing animals to fight humans or each other. Some bloodsports are banned in certain regions but others are not. For example, cockfighting, where two roosters fight each other (sometimes with sharp blades attached to their legs) is banned in North America and Europe, but remains popular in Central America and the Philippines. Other gruesome bloodsports, like bear-baiting (where dogs attack chained bears), are not as popular.

Bear-baiting still persists, however, in remote parts of Pakistan. A bear, sometimes with its canine teeth removed and front claws filed down, is restrained by a rope or chain in the middle of a makeshift arena. While spectators watch, fighting dogs are released. They leap and bite while the bear tries to defend itself. Bear-baiting seems to be in decline in Pakistan due to the efforts of animal welfare groups like the World Society for the Protection of Animals.

Horse-fighting is a somewhat popular sport in parts of the Philippines, although it is actually illegal. Two stallions are encouraged to fight over a mare in season. The horses bite, kick and strike at each other. Wounds and broken bones can result. Some fights are even covered on local television. Fans of horse-fighting claim it's a traditional activity but it seems to be more about gambling than anything else.

Dog-fighting: Duel to the Death

One of the most despicable forms of animal-based entertainment is dog-fighting. Heavily muscled dogs attack each other in a ring or pit, while audience members place bets on which dog will win. The dogs suffer deep cuts, torn skin, punctured eyes, ripped ears, and a range of other injuries. It's no surprise that many of them don't live very long.

Training a fighting dog may involve even more cruelty because smaller dogs are often provided for the fighters to practice on. Those unfortunate and terrified animals suffer tremendously.

Dog-fighting is banned in many areas but persists as a widespread underground, illegal activity because some people seem to enjoy seeing dogs rip each other apart.

Bullfighting

Bullfights take place in the European countries of Spain, France, and Portugal, and in the Latin American countries of Mexico, Venezuela, Ecuador, Colombia and Peru. In some areas, they attract thousands of spectators. According to the World Society for the Protection of Animals, about 250,000 bulls are killed each year in the bullfighting industry.

The most famous dog-fighter is Michael Vick, a professional football player. In July 2007, Vick and three other men were charged with conducting a six year dog-fighting operation called Bad Newz Kennels. Vick was charged with financing the operation, participating in dog-fights, and executing unwanted dogs. On December 10, 2007, he was sentenced to 23 months in a US federal prison and ordered to pay more than $1 million to care for confiscated dogs. Michael Vick is now speaking out against dog-fighting.

More than 45 towns and cities in Spain have declared themselves to be anti-bullfighting.

CAS/Sabine Joosten

Spanish-style bullfights have three stages. First the bull is confronted by the matador. Then a picador mounted on a horse stabs a lance into the mound of muscle on the bull's neck to weaken the animal. In the second stage, banderilleros jab razor sharp, barbed sticks near the wound made by the picador. The final stage involves the matador reentering the ring with a small red cape and a sword. The weakened bull attempts to charge the matador who moves out of the way. Eventually the bull is fatally stabbed.

In Portuguese-style bullfights people try to snatch a decorative rosette from the bull's head or leap over the bull. They're not as bloody as the Spanish-style, but once a fight is over the bull is usually killed.

Bulls suffer when they are taunted and slowly killed. With growing criticism of the sport, there seems little doubt that bullfighting will eventually end or at least change. Hopefully that time will come soon.

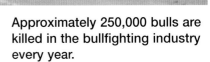

Approximately 250,000 bulls are killed in the bullfighting industry every year.

CAS/Sabine Joosten

Cute, Funny, but Oh-So-Dangerous

While I was writing this chapter, a Moscow Circus "ice skating" bear killed circus administrator Dmitry Popatov and seriously injured a trainer who tried to rescue him. A short time later, a killer whale at Sea World killed a trainer by pulling her into his tank. In April 2008, a handler at California-based Predators in Action, a company that trains animals for films, was attacked and killed by a five-year-old grizzly bear, previously known to be a calm, gentle animal.

Many animals in entertainment are dangerous because they're large or powerful, or possess teeth and claws capable of inflicting

TRACS/ <http://www.tracs-bc.ca-www.tracs-bc.ca

serious injury. They are often housed, handled, and moved without adequate safety measures in place. They may even be walked from one location to another on a leash. The potential for escape or attack can be very high.

On October 3, 2003 in Las Vegas, audience members at the Siegfried & Roy show watched in horror as a seven-year-old white tiger, Montecore, critically injured Roy Horn by biting him on the neck. Montecore had been performing since he was six months old. The show was immediately shut down. Roy, who now walks with a cane, is lucky to be alive.

In February 2001 in Pennsylvania, a tiger mauled a trainer with more than 30 years experience. A 20-year-old circus worker was mauled to death by three tigers during a show in West Bengal, India in 2000. Animal trainer Joy Holiday died in October 1998 after being attacked by a tiger from her show, Ron and Joy Holiday's Cat Dancers. The tiger killed another trainer approximately one month later.

In February 2009, former performing chimpanzee Travis inflicted massive injuries on a friend of his keeper. Chimps can live to be 60 years old. Travis was only 15 when police shot him dead.

Every year elephants injure or kill handlers or bystanders. In 2007, a 50-year-old elephant at an Australian circus crushed a handler to death. Just a week earlier, an elephant in an Indian circus pulled down a circus tent and attacked the ticket counters. In January 2005, while being loaded onto a truck, a 36-year-old female elephant trampled a circus trainer to death. In Hawaii in 1994, Tyke the elephant killed her trainer during a performance, injured another worker, escaped, and rampaged through the streets of Kaka'ako. Police shot Tyke more than 80 times before she died.

Trainers and show operators almost always say they treat animals kindly and that they keep them under control at all times. But the ever-growing number of incidents tells a different story. Audience members and bystanders are often at risk when they're around performing animals, but most of them don't even know it.

When the Show Ends

When animals become too old, ill or dangerous, they don't generate income, so they may be discarded and end up in very poor homes. Some of these "retired" animals even find themselves in circumstances where they continue to be exploited for profit.

Walter the chimp is thought to have been part of a traveling zoo as a baby; later he was used in a television series. He was retired to the Amarillo Wildlife Refuge (AWR) in Texas. In 2003, an undercover PETA investigator found Walter living in a barren cement enclosure, next to piles of rotten food and excrement. He had little to do except lie on a soiled, garbage-strewn platform, or squabble with the other chimps who shared his tiny space. Another young male chimp named Chubbs, who had once been in the movie *Planet of the Apes*, lived in similar conditions at AWR.

© Captive Animals' Protection Society

After his performing career ended, Fred the bear was confined in a small, concrete-floored cage. His frustration and boredom often led him to bite the bars of his cage.

Adult chimpanzees like Walter and Chubbs are impossible to handle safely, but they are often kept for breeding. Baby chimps are used in film productions and photo shoots or sold for a profit.

Shortly after the PETA investigation, Walter was transferred to another facility. In 2005, AWR owner Charles Azzopardi was caught trying to sell endangered clouded leopards to a buyer in Oklahoma. He was charged with illegal trafficking of endangered animals across state lines. In 2006, he received a $2,000 fine, 180 days of home confinement and 3 years probation. And then in March 2008, his license to keep animals was suspended for two years.

CASE STUDY: Oso the Bear

Oso was probably born in the backcountry of Alaska. He stayed close to his mother, until the day she was shot by a hunter. Oso ended up in a Canadian circus. His front teeth and claws were removed. When the circus closed down, he was sold to a zoo. When the zoo also closed, the owners left Oso trapped in his cage. Three weeks later, he was dehydrated, starving and close to death. It's a wonder he survived.

Oso was moved to a facility in southern Ontario and regained his health. A major fire led to his transfer to a private animal collection. Oso was again neglected and his weight dropped to 136 kg (300 lbs). He was emaciated, starving and barely able to stand.

Oso's previous caretakers intervened and arranged for him to go to the Bear With Us sanctuary where he lived in a 3,716 sq m (40,000 sq ft) forested enclosure. Owner Michael McIntosh, said, "He's been through so much. Yet, he's the most congenial, gentle and friendly animal I've ever worked with. Sometimes I sit under a tree and just talk to him. He seems so

contented." On August 17, 2000, at the very young age of 15, Oso passed away. Michael thinks Oso's years of abuse shortened his life.

CHAPTER 6

New Directions for Performing Animals

Animal-Free Circuses

I'll never forget the first time I saw a Cirque de Soleil performance. The lights dimmed, lush music filled the tent, and circus performers in fantastic costumes, danced onto the stage and performed flawlessly. They were amazing. It was the most incredible circus I'd ever seen—and there wasn't an animal in sight.

Cirque de Soleil has become one of the biggest circus producers, and they now promote shows around the world. There are dozens of other theatrical circuses too, including small shows with just a few performers, youth circuses, acrobatic troupes and large, big budget stage circuses. Their numbers are growing because they're fun and entertaining, and that's what circuses are all about.

http://flickr.com/photo/85128884@N00/2650981813

Computer-Generated Animals

The blockbuster movie *King Kong* was released in 2005. A giant computer-generated gorilla was the main character. A friend of mine who studies gorillas in the wild said King Kong not only looked real, but moved like a real gorilla, too. Amazing!

When I first saw the computer-generated dinosaurs in *Jurassic Park*, I left the theatre wondering how such incredibly real-looking dinosaurs could be created. I've since watched dozens of movies and shows featuring simulated animal characters, including lifelike computer-generated images (CGI) and animatronic creatures (like Willy, the killer whale in the *Free Willy* movies). They all looked true-to-life.

In June 2009, I had a remarkable encounter with—amazingly—a *Tyrannosaurus rex*. I sat quietly as the enormous animal "walked" past me, making deep rumbling sounds. It could have been a tense, dangerous situation, except I was at *Walking with Dinosaurs–The Live Experience,* and of course, the T-rex wasn't real. The show, which took place in a darkened arena, featured more than a dozen lifelike, life-size dinosaurs. Thanks to this show, millions of people around the world have had their own dinosaur encounter.

The technologies available today are amazing and getting better all the time. The astonishing creatures in the movie *Avatar* show that it's possible to create any kind of animal—real or imaginary. With so many alternatives, there's no reason to use live animals anymore.

Sanctuaries and Rescue Centers

Sanctuaries and rescue centers provide refuge for unwanted, abused and abandoned animals and bring attention to their plight. Unfortunately, space is limited, so only a tiny fraction of the animals now used in entertainment can be taken in.

Center for Great Apes

Center for Great Apes

The Center for Great Apes in Wauchula, Florida is the only sanctuary in the United States for chimpanzees and orangutans from the entertainment and pet industry. Patti Ragan founded the sanctuary after working with orphaned orangutans in Borneo and an infant orangutan in the US. Twelve large, domed enclosures connected by 4,000 feet of elevated steel tunnels provide a complex environment equipped with climbing apparatus, swinging vines, objects to manipulate, room to roam and the companionship of other apes.

CASE STUDY: Sammy the Film Star

Born in 1989, Sammy the orangutan spent his first 18 months at a Miami tourist attraction owned by an orangutan breeder. He was then sold, along with infant Geri, to a Hollywood animal trainer. Sammy and Geri grew up together and were used for commercials and television shows. Sammy also starred in several movies, including *Dunston Checks In* (he was Dunstan). As Sammy matured he became dangerous to handle, so he was retired to a small cage at the trainer's compound. In 2004, Sammy and Geri were sent to the Center for Great Apes in Florida. Their son Jam arrived four months later. They now enjoy a better life in roomy, complex surroundings.

The Mona Foundation

The Mona Foundation was set up to provide a home to illegally imported chimpanzees rescued from beach photographers in Spain. At the Mona Foundation, chimps live in natural environment enclosures with climbing structures, lookout points and extensive areas of grassland. The Foundation also conducts campaigns aimed at ending the exploitation of animals in the entertainment industry.

CASE STUDY: Marco the Chimpanzee

Marco was born on July 4, 1984 in Spain. He was taken from his mother shortly after birth. He spent most of his time locked in a small cage with other young chimpanzees and became famous by starring in several TV commercials for large Spanish companies, such as Telefonica and Estrella Damm beer. When he and the other chimps were 8 to 10 years old, they were too strong to control, so they were locked in a dilapidated truck in a vacant lot. They were confined in pairs in cages so small they could barely stand up. They couldn't socialize or do anything chimpanzees normally do and were in darkness most of the time. For more than eight years, they sat in filthy cages, with no physical activity and a poor diet, enduring the suffocating heat of summer and the cold of winter. Marco developed heart disease.

In 2001 the Mona Foundation rescued Marco and the other chimps. In his new spacious surroundings Marco became relaxed and playful; he now comforts the other chimps when they're frightened. Marco can finally act like a real chimpanzee.

Mona Foundation/FUNDACIÓ MONA

Performing Animal Welfare Society (PAWS)

Performing Animal Welfare Society

Working in television in the 1970s, Hollywood animal trainer Pat Derby discovered widespread neglect and abuse. In 1984 she and her partner Ed Stewart founded PAWS and began working for laws to protect animals in entertainment. Today PAWS operates three California sanctuaries that provide hundreds of animals, including a growing herd of elephants, with a lifetime home. One of their sanctuaries is the 2,300 acre "ARK 2000" in San Andreas, California.

Romanian Bear Sanctuary

Romanian Bear Sanctuary

The Romanian Bear Sanctuary provides refuge for bears rescued from cramped, filthy conditions where they were starved and tormented to entertain tourists. There are 34 bears now living at the sanctuary, including two blind bears named Max and Ursula. Their spacious, natural paddocks let them engage in real bear behaviors. An education program teaches local people about the bears, why they are important, and why all bears should be protected.

Fred, the Last Circus Bear in Britain

Fred the bear spent his life performing simple, silly tricks. He wore a leather and metal muzzle on his face and lived in a tiny barren beast wagon. In 1998, the Captive Animals' Protection Society (CAPS) launched a campaign to free him. Their campaign attracted national attention. In 2001, the circus started to sell some of its animals, but Fred remained at their base in a small, concrete-floored cage.

CAPS didn't give up. In 2003, the circus agreed to let Fred go. In December he was flown to the Bear With Us sanctuary in Canada. For the first time in his life, Fred had room to roam, grass, trees and sunshine.

CHAPTER 7
A World with No Dancing Bears

It's easy to become overwhelmed by the many, complex problems faced by animals in entertainment. But people are speaking out, old abusive practices are gradually being eliminated, laws are being passed, and the lives of many animals are improving. Every day I hear about new projects and campaigns, many of them started by individuals and small groups of people working with few resources. They learned about a problem and decided to do something about it.

The Photo Chimps

For years, Singapore Zoo visitors could have their photo taken with a baby chimpanzee. The photo chimps lived in cages away from their family group. Once they became powerful adults and could no longer be used in photo sessions, many were shipped to other Asian or Middle Eastern zoos.

Rob Laidlaw

In addition to helping baby chimps, ACRES established Singapore's first wildlife rescue center.

Louis Ng, a student in Singapore, was concerned. He knew that separating babies from their mothers was traumatic for both. He wondered what happened to the chimps who were sent to other zoos. He started an investigation. His findings led to a campaign to stop the photo sessions.

Louis went on to establish ACRES (Animal Concerns Research and Education Society). ACRES initiated an exhaustive investigation into the fate of the exported zoo chimps and discovered many in horrible situations. ACRES then persuaded the Singapore Zoo to make changes to their protocol for sending animals to other zoos. By working closely with several of the zoos that received Singapore Zoo chimps, ACRES also managed to improve their living conditions. It was a very successful campaign.

Playing with Tigers: Exposing the Tiger Temple

A 2004 *Animal Planet* show generated worldwide attention for the Thai Tiger Temple in Kanchanaburi, Thailand. Images of monks living freely with tigers and tourists playing with the cats made the Temple famous. By 2007, the place received hundreds of visitors daily.

Each afternoon Temple staff brought tigers on chain leashes into an area called the Tiger Canyon. The tigers were then held for three hours by 3m (9.8 ft)–5m (16.4 ft) chains. Temple staff remained close to each tiger when visitors were present.

The first eight tigers came to the Temple in 1999 or 2000. It didn't take long for complaints to reach wildlife protection groups, like Care for the Wild International (CWI). Visitors reported tigers being punched, kicked, and beaten, their tails pulled, and urine sprayed in their faces (wild tigers use urine spraying as a territorial or aggressive signal).

CWI investigated. They discovered tigers housed in small, barren, concrete and iron cages most of the time. In late 2007, a few of the tigers were moved into a larger 80–100m² (861–1076 sq. ft) outdoor space. The Temple was also breeding its tigers. Between 2003 and 2006, one tiger had seven litters of cubs. Other females also had litters. CWI uncovered evidence that tigers had been illegally exported to a neighboring country. The trafficking of tiger parts across international borders is a big threat to the survival of all tigers.

Now tourists know the Temple isn't the tiger-friendly place they thought it was. CWI is pushing for the confiscation of the Temple tigers and their relocation to a sanctuary.

India's Last Dancing Bear

In December 2009 one of the last dancing bears was rescued from the streets of India. His name is Raju and he was surrendered to Wildlife SOS at their bear rescue center in southern India. The rope that had been inserted through Raju's face, that caused him years of misery, was surgically removed. Now Raju

These tigers are from the Tiger Temple of Wat Phra Luang Ta Bua, Kanchanaburi Province, Thailand.

can enjoy a peaceful life in a spacious natural pen for as long as he lives.

With assistance from the Indian Ministry of Environment and Forests and state forest departments, Wildlife SOS and a coalition of international wildlife protection organizations initiated a program that resulted in 600 of India's dancing bears being surrendered over a seven-year period.

Dancing bears have been a part of India for 400 years. To encourage the surrender of bears, owners were given rehabilitation packages that allow them to learn new professions and ensure that their children get an education.

The rescue and retirement of India's dancing bears into a network of Wildlife SOS sanctuaries is a remarkable achievement. The fact that the project was successful shows just what can be accomplished when people set their mind to it.

Crayfish and Elephants

The New Zealand animal protection group SAFE has had some great success helping animals in entertainment. One of their campaigns involved an elephant named Jumbo.

For 30 years Jumbo lived out of the back of a truck in the circus. In 2004, SAFE dedicated itself to freeing Jumbo from circus life. In 2005, they staged 40 protests and in the years that followed they continued to apply pressure by generating awareness and media interest in Jumbo's plight. In just 6 months in 2009, SAFE held another 35 protests.

The campaign worked, Jumbo was freed and she now lives at the Franklin Zoo and Wildlife Sanctuary in conditions far removed from those in the circus. For the first time in more than 30 years Jumbo has access to indoor and outdoor living space, sand hills, rubbing posts, mud wallows, a place to forage and many of the other things that every elephant needs. In the future, SAFE hopes to send Jumbo to a world-renowned elephant sanctuary with even more space to roam and other elephants to socialize with.

In 1999, SAFE also rescued two circus chimpanzees named

Crayfish are timid shellfish, preferring to hide under rocks and leaves.

Buddy and Sonny. Both of them now live in semi-natural conditions in the largest chimp sanctuary in Africa where they can finally act like chimps should.

A few years before that, SAFE campaigned against the Great International Moscow Circus that featured a whole menagerie of animals, including skating bears. The SAFE campaign decreased ticket sales, so the circus promoter launched a lawsuit against the group to recover costs, but was unsuccessful. No international circus has visited New Zealand since then.

If that wasn't enough, SAFE also successfully fought an odd arcade machine, called Catcha Cray, in which people could try to pick up a live crayfish like they would a stuffed toy. Some of the animals were caught dozens of times, a very stressful process, before being dragged out of the machine. The SAFE campaign resulted in a number of the machines being removed from bars in the City of Auckland and then, in cooperation with the Auckland and Royal New Zealand SPCAs, all of the machines being removed.

A FINAL WORD

It's not always easy making change happen and it sometimes takes a long time. Try to stay positive.

You won't always win. Sometimes you'll have to figure out a new approach and try again. If you're dedicated, you'll keep working toward your goal, and you'll learn valuable lessons from the setbacks you encounter along the way.

Recognize that big changes don't always happen. Sometimes when you work for change, it moves slowly in small steps. But every step forward is a step you can be proud of. You can start by reading the *Ten Ways You Can Help Animals in Entertainment* that I've listed in the next section of this book.

There are many animals that need your help, so don't delay. You really can make a difference.

Ten Ways to Help Animals in Entertainment

1 Learn as much as you can about animals in entertainment and how they are treated. Start by contacting the organizations listed at the back of this book for more information.

2 Go to movies that use computer generated images of animals or models, instead of movies that use live animals.

3 Avoid live animal shows, including dolphin shows, Swim-With-The-Dolphin programs, animal photo sessions, animal rides and contests where animals are used as prizes.

4 Don't go to circuses or shows that feature live animal performances. Support non-animal entertainment instead.

5 Inform your family, friends and colleagues about the mistreatment and abuse of performing animals. Ask them not to support live animal entertainment businesses.

6 Start writing letters to newspapers, magazines, government agencies, politicians and the companies that profit from live animal entertainment. Let them know you oppose what they are doing and why.

7 Create a website, Facebook or MySpace page or start a blog. Create a display at your school that shows how performing animals suffer and why everyone should work to end their exploitation for entertainment.

8 Start a campaign to make your school or club animal-friendly or to get a performing animal prohibition in your community. Make sure no animal shows are invited to make a presentation at your school. Start an Animal Club and get more kids involved.

9 Visit an accredited sanctuary that helps unwanted, abused or retired performing animals. Do some research in advance, because there are lots of phony sanctuaries.

10 Join an animal protection group that works to end the exploitation of animals in entertainment.

Arguments and Answers

Why would animal trainers abuse their animals?

If animals don't perform when required, they become a liability. Instead of generating money, they cost money, so trainers have a strong incentive to make animals perform.

Why would animals do tricks if they were abused?

Performing animals may be trained using intimidation, physical punishment or other inappropriate methods. The animals submit and follow directions because they know what will happen if they don't.

The animals performing look okay, so what makes you so sure they're being abused?

Looks can be deceiving. All animals require more than food, water and a tiny living space to thrive. They need natural spaces, freedom of choice, a proper social group, and things to do or they become bored, frustrated and stressed. Their health may get worse and abnormal behaviors, like pacing, head bobbing, and bar biting, often develop. Since most people only see animals when they're performing, they don't realize what their lives are like behind the scenes.

Environment and Animal Ethics Group (EAEG)

Aren't most performing animals born in captivity?

No, many performing animals come from the wild. For example, many of the elephants in North American circuses were born in the wild. A 1994 investigation by a group called TRAFFIC revealed that European circuses often trade in wild-caught apes, bears, elephants and other species. In Thailand, a substantial number of orangutans in zoo shows came from the wild.

Don't performing animal acts help educate children about animals and the environment?

No, most animals in entertainment do nothing more than serve as props or perform simple, silly tricks. Since they can't act naturally, there is little that can be learned by watching them. You can't find out anything about their real lives in the wild, including how they move about their home range, find mates, avoid threats, care for their young, communicate with family and friends, solve problems, build nests and shelters, hunt or forage for food, or any of the other things that animals do. At most, you can learn a few simple animal facts that could easily be found in a book or on the internet, and see their size, shape and color, but even these are often different from their wild relatives. Worse yet, after seeing animals in entertainment, many people may think it's okay to use animals that way or to keep them as pets.

Don't the laws protect animals?

Many laws are poorly written and difficult to enforce. Penalties are often very light. Some laws only deal with abuse that causes severe injury or death. They almost never deal with an animal's need for space, freedom of choice, a proper social group or things to do.

There are laws in some areas that prohibit wild animals in circuses and other entertainment situations, but we need more of them.

Some people in the entertainment industry say the laws are already too tough and restrictive. But how tough can they be when elephants can still be chained and big cats kept in beast wagons for most of their lives? I don't think the laws are anywhere near tough enough.

How can I help prevent the mistreatment and abuse of performing animals?

The best thing you can do is refuse to support businesses that use live animals. Also, check out *Ten Ways to Help Animals in Entertainment* on page 47. If you do even one thing on the list, you'll help a lot of animals. Try to do the whole list and you'll help even more.

Rob Laidlaw

Organizations to Contact

Animal Defenders International
www.ad-international.org

Animals Australia
www.animalsaustralia.org

Bear With Us
www.bearwithus.org

Born Free Foundation
www.bornfree.org.uk, www.bornfreeusa.org

Captive Animals' Protection Society
www.captiveanimals.org

Care for the Wild International
www.careforthewild.org

CAS International
www.cas-international.org/en

Center for Great Apes
www.centerforgreatapes.org

Compassion Unlimited Plus Action
www.cupabangalore.org

Fauna Foundation
www.faunafoundation.org

Greyhound Protection League
www.greyhounds.org

Grey2K USA
www.GREY2KUSA.org

Humane Society of the United States
www.humanesociety.org

One Voice
http://www.one-voice.fr/en

People for the Ethical Treatment of Animals
www.peta.org, www.petaindia.com
www.circuses.com

Performing Animal Welfare Society
www.pawsweb.org

SAFE
www.safe.org.nz

Say No to Animals in Circuses
www.animalcircuses.com

Shambala Preserve/ Roar Foundation
www.shambala.org

The Mona Foundation
www.fundacionmona.org/en/

World Society for the Protection of Animals
www.wspa.org.uk

Zoocheck Canada
www.zoocheck.com

Glossary

Abnormal Behavior: A behavior, such as repetitive pacing or sleeping all the time, that doesn't typically occur in a normal animal, especially in the wild.

Ankus: A hand-held tool with a sharp point and hook on one end that is used to prod an animal, such as an elephant.

Animal welfare: The physical and psychological state of animals as they attempt to cope with their environment.

Animatronic: A technology in which electronics are used to make animal puppets and models move and appear alive.

Beast wagon: A wheeled wagon that is used to transport animals.

Bloodsport: A sport in which animals are forced to fight each other or humans, often to the death.

Computer Generated Image (CGI): Animated graphics produced on a computer that are used in movies and other kinds of films.

Metabolism: The physical and chemical processes in an animal that are necessary for the maintenance of life.

Performing animal: An animal that is used in any kind of performance in a circus, show, or presentation for the entertainment of humans.

Sanctuary: A facility that provides a lifetime home to abused and unwanted animals. It doesn't breed, sell or exploit animals for entertainment or profit.

Stress: A physical, psychological, or emotional strain that causes tension and discomfort. It can be a factor in disease and suffering.

SWTD: A program in which paying customers enter the water to touch or swim with a captive dolphin.

Theatrical circus: A circus performed on a stage instead of in a ring.

Ungulate: A mammal with hooves, such as a horse, zebra, camel or rhinoceros.

Index

Praise for *On Parade: The Hidden World of Animals in Entertainment*

"After working for many years with Nancy Burnet, of United Activists for Animal Rights, exposing cruelty to animals in entertainment, I can assure you that such cruelty is rampant. Rob Laidlaw's book, "On Parade," tells the tragic story of animal suffering for man's diversion in vivid, heartbreaking detail. Read it, and help us save these pitiful creatures from the clutches of those who would do them harm."
—*Bob Barker, Television personality and activist*

"Animals are used in a wide variety of ways solely for human entertainment, and many of these individuals are severely abused in the process. Rob Laidlaw's book is essential reading for those interested in animal protection and humane education and for those who want to learn more about these subjects. Children are the ambassadors for a more peaceful and compassionate future and this book provides essential information so that they and others will come to respect other animals and do what's needed to grant them the protection they want and deserve."
—*Marc Bekoff, author of* The Emotional Lives of Animals, Animals Matter, Animals at Play, and The Animal Manifesto: Six Reasons for Expanding our Compassion Footprint.

"Rob Laidlaw exposes the cruel, profit-driven underbelly of the animal entertainment industry. This is must-reading for anyone considering a trip to the circus, the zoo, or the aquarium."
–*Jonathan Balcombe, author of* Second Nature: The Inner Lives of Animals

"To change the world of tomorrow we need to educate the kids of today—a simple, no-nonsense look at the use of animals in many forms of 'entertainment'. Looking beyond the usual topics of zoos and circuses, Rob also exposes the cruelties in greyhound and horse racing, animal use in films, and photo sessions. When future generations end the captivity and brutality of animals for entertainment, Rob's books will be seen as an essential part of that process."
–*Craig Redmond, Campaigns Director, Captive Animals' Protection Society (CAPS) www.captiveanimals.org*

"Wonderful, solid, educational and absorbing. This book gives every young reader a lesson in our evolving idea of who animals are and our obligations to respect them."
–*Ingrid Newkirk, President, People for the Ethical Treatment of Animals*

"This is a wonderful book that uses real life stories to expose the dark side of what many people still think of as family-oriented leisure and entertainment activities. Although aimed at children, this book is an educational must-read for parents who take their children to circuses, animal exhibits, and other events where animals are on parade."
—*Silia Smith, Regional Director, Canada, World Society for the Protection of Animals*

"Rob Laidlaw's has written an important story because it concerns the costs to performing animals—often deliberately hidden—of amusing humans."
—*Anne Russon, PhD. Primatologist. Author of* Orangutans: Wizards of the Rainforest

"Rob Laidlaw's important new book *On Parade* paints a detailed picture of the many unseen ways in which animals suffer when they are used in entertainment and advertising. Laidlaw does the hard work of explaining—in detailed, simple, calm terms—why an animal that looks OK on display (or in a photo, or on TV) is inherently living an unnatural and often miserable quality of life. The greatest hope for humane treatment of animals in the future is that the current generation of children will be raised with an entirely different set of expectations about what is acceptable."
—*Camilla Calamandrei, documentary filmmaker* The Tiger Next Door

"*On Parade* is a compelling children's book that challenges children to put themselves in the place of animals in the entertainment industry and to ask themselves, "Would I like to live like this?" Clearly the answer is no. Laidlaw then gently guides children to the informational tools they need to make change in their world for abused entertainment animals."
—*Else Poulsen, Zoological Consultant and Author of* Smiling Bears— A Zookeeper Explores the Behavior and Emotional Life of Bears

"*On Parade* educates children about the realities of life for millions of animals throughout the world who are confined, used and abused for our viewing pleasures. [This book] will help young growing minds make informed decisions about their own willingness to participate—even as an observer—in the animals' suffering. Laidlaw gives his readers an experience that will help them grow into the kind of person who will want to, will be able to, and will help change the world."
—*Gloria Grow, founder of the Fauna Foundation chimpanzee sanctuary*

54

Praise for *Wild Animals in Captivity*

Nominated for the Ontario Library Association Silver Birch Award for Non-Fiction

"Rob Laidlaw has been working tirelessly on behalf of animals in zoos ever since I met him many years ago. This well-written book, with its carefully chosen examples and photographs, is a fair assessment of what is bad, better, and best for animals in this world of captivity. It will help you to judge for yourself whether or not the conditions are suitable so that, when necessary, you can speak out on behalf of some unhappy animal prisoner."
—*Dr. Jane Goodall, DBE, Founder, the Jane Goodall Institute, UN Messenger of Peace*

"Laidlaw presents a passionate, well-written, and well-researched argument against the practices of most zoos around the world…The issues raised in the important and powerful book will resonate with young and old."
—*School Library Journal* Book of the Year Selection, 2008

"Illustrated with eye-catching color photography throughout, *Wild Animals in Captivity* encourages young readers to think long and hard about zoos…Highly recommended."
—*Midwest Book Review*

"*Wild Animals in Captivity* is a well designed, thorough, yet concise depiction of life for animals in captivity. Laidlaw's balanced presentation not only focuses on examples of inhumane treatment of animals in zoos but also gives instances of the best. Highly Recommended"
—*CM Magazine*

"[This] is a great book that not only explains the problems of keeping wild animals in captivity in an easy to understand and entertaining way, it also provides ways for the reader to make a difference and help the animals themselves."
—*Dave Eastham, Head of Wildlife, World Society for the Protection of Animals*

"With the natural world fast disappearing, [this book] offers a timely and very important look at why, where, and how we need to change our treatment of wild animals. It aims to help youngsters understand what life is like for wild animals in zoos, including showing readers how to see for themselves. Laidlaw offers a fair, balanced assessment that is easy to read and engagingly illustrated with real stories and pictures. For anyone planning a zoo visit, old or young, I'd put *Wild Animals in Captivity* on their must-read list."
—*Anne E. Russon PhD, Author,* Orangutans, Wizards of the Rainforest *and* Reaching into Thought: The Minds of the Great Apes

"Most kids love to visit zoos and enjoy seeing animals. This book takes such visits to another level by giving children, their parents, and teachers the ability to assess zoos and the well-being of the animals they house. With a balanced, fair approach, the text explains what happens to so many of the cute baby animals we see in zoos; whether or not endangered species are being protected; whether or not the animals are hurt or helped by their experiences; and how zoos can help or hurt individual animals in their care. There is nothing else like it; [this book] should be read by all kids and adults planning a trip to the zoo."
—*Barry Kent MacKay, Ornithological Artist; Naturalist; Author; Senior Program Associate, Born Free USA*

"At last—a book for young people about animals that tells it like it is. With stark common sense, Laidlaw lays out the evidence that wildlife belongs in the wild. Whitewashing captivity has been the norm for too long—we now know too much to continue to ignore the suffering of the complex animals we incarcerate. The zoo community won't like this book, but with the scientific and experiential substantiation, it won't be able to deny its legitimate place in the genre."
—*Debra Probert, Executive Director, Vancouver Humane Society*

"If there ever was a book that taught empathy, compassion, and respect for our fellow beings, that captured the spirit and essence of the varied species with whom we share our planet, this [book] is certainly it. Through personal stories and observations, Rob Laidlaw has beautifully juxtaposed the quality of the lives of animals in the wild to those in captivity. This splendid book will open up the hearts, minds, and awareness of its readers, young and old, to the beauty of animals, and to the terrible plight of so many of them in captivity. Beautifully, we are educated as to the ways their lives can and should be improved. It is clearly one of the best books on animals, be they in the wild or in captivity, that I have ever read. Its clear information and powerful message must spread to young and old alike."
—*Elliot M. Katz, DVM President, In Defense of Animals*